SAP Basis Interview Questions, Answers, and Explanations

By Equity Press

Please visit our website at www.sapcookbook.com

ISBN 0-9753052-9-8

The programs in this book have been included for instructional value only. They have been tested with care but are not guaranteed for any particular purpose. The publisher does not offer any warranties or representations not does it accept any liabilities with respect to the programs.

Trademark notices

Motivation

During the course of an average project, I am usually called upon by a project manager to "help screen resources" for different parts of the project. And one thing comes to mind – if done properly, it's very time consuming, and it's really hard work!

My interviews usually sound something like this –

Jim: "Please rate yourself, on a scale of 1-10 on your SAP Basis knowledge and experience..."

Interviewee: "Um, probably something like 10..."

Jim: "OK, so, let me just say something... I don't believe there is such a thing as a ten."

Interviewee: "What would you rate yourself?"

Jim: "I rate myself an 8."

Interviewee: "Why so low?"

Jim: "There's no such thing as a ten. All of the nines are working at SAP, SAP Labs, or SAP Consulting, and so basically that puts me at about an eight. But we're here to talk about **your** skills. And so you think you're a 10, huh? OK, so tell me what you know about debugging the n-step approval workflow..."

And then I try to ask the questions that truly flesh out a person's understanding of the software. It's part science, part art to be sure – but the #1 thing I'm looking for in an interview is that the resource represents their skills truthfully. The good resources know what they know, know what they don't know, and they're open about it.

And so I hope that this book will serve as a much-needed guide for managers trying to get the right resource for their project. If you construct an interview based on these questions, I'm confident you can get a good idea about the depth and breadth of a consultant's experiences and accumulated knowledge.

Jim Stewart

Riverside, California

August 2005

Introduction

This book is divided into three parts – configuration related questions, technical and troubleshooting questions, and finally, a very long list of transaction codes and tables that apply to the area of SAP Basis.

Each interview question has a question and an answer – that is pretty straightforward – but when you see the guru icon – this is information that represents the highest degree of knowledge in a particular area. So f you're looking for a "Basis guru" be sure to listen for an answers similar to those given under the guru icon.

 Don't be bamboozled!

The Basis Guru has Spoken!

Question 1: Transport Change Request

If your SAP landscape is composed of a DEV server and PRD server and you need to transport a change request from DEV client 111 to DEV 131 (i.e. transport in the same server). How can this be accomplished?

A: Transaction SCC1

Question 2: Internet outages

We have recently experienced some internet outages caused by our ISP. Although we have resolved our ISP problems, the users refuse to believe that losing the internet connection was to blame for the SAP problems. How can we ensure that this was an internet problem and not an SAP problem?

A: Open a maintenance window, connect to the machine and kill the ISP connection and see if this kills your connection. Repeat at will until they believe that the ISP was the problem.

Question 3: OK Codes

What is an OK code? What are the differences an OK code to a T-code?

A: An OK Code is used by a program to execute a function for example after a pushbutton has been clicked. A transaction code is a "shortcut" that helps a user run a program.

 T-Codes are stored in table TSTC

Question 4: Transaction Codes

Where are t-code name and program values stored? How can I find a list of all the t-codes in the SAP system?

A: You can use transaction st11 to view Table TSTC. You can define a new t-code using transaction se93.

Question 5: STMS Importing

How can one disable the "Import All" button on STMS for the queues?

A: Login to your Transport Domain Controller. Run STMS->Overview->System. Choose the System you want to disable import all. Go to Transport Tool tab. Add/Create Parameter "NO_IMPORT_ALL" set its value to 1.

Question 6: Work Processes

What are the different types of work processes in R/3?

A: Dialog (D), Update (U), Enqueue (E), Background(B), and Spool(S).

Question 7: Patch Level for GUI

How can you confirm the patch level for SAP GUI?

A: Log into SAPGUI, and hit Alt-F12 -> About

Question 8: Web help installation

Why can web help be considered easier to install than CHM, the standard delivered SAP help?

A: Web help is easier than trying to get every remote user connected to a network share. If you don't want to use SAP's help site, you can setup your own website to do it. The best route depends on your business' network structure.

Question 9: Web Resources

If you can't find the answer to a question, what are some website you can visit to find the answer?

A:

OSS notes: http://service.sap.com/notes
SAP help: http://help.sap.com
Google: http://www.google.com

Question 10: Instance installation

We want to install another new instance on same development box. Is this possible? What are some of the important considerations?

A: Yes, it is possible to have more than one instance on a single box. The key is to use a different SID and a different system number. It is also important to note that for a 64 bit SAP kernel, SAP recommends a 20 GB swap space for 1st instance and 10 GB per each additional instance.

Question 11: Client copy

What is the difference between a client copy and client refresh?

A: Some times these are the same, For example, if you are performing a copy to an existing client for the express purpose of updating the data, then it is called Client Refresh.

If you are copying to a newly created client then it is more appropriate to say "client copy."

Another way of thinking about this is that a client copy from production to a QA server or from production to DEV server is really a client refresh.

Question 12: Table T000

What is the purpose of table T000?

A: Table T000 contains a list of defined clients, which you can maintain with transaction SCC4.

Question 13: Table USR02

What is the purpose of table USR02?

A: This table stores User IDs and passwords.

Question 14: Passwords

How do you create a password exception list?

A: Place the answers in table USR40.

Question 15: Table TADIR

What is the purpose of table TADIR?

A: Table TADIR contains object directory entries.

Question 16: Table TDEVC

What is the purpose of table TDEVC?

A: Table TDEVC contains development classes and packages.

Question 17: Change Requests

What are the transaction codes associated with changing requests, request headers, or request object lists?

A: The following tables hold information about change requesets.

E070	Change request headers
E071	Change request object lists

Question 18: User Access

How can you get a list of the users with development access on a particular system?

A: Table DEVACCESS

Question 19: Transport object keys

Where can you find a list of object keys included in a transport?

A: E071K Object keys contained within transports

Question 20: Transport in progress

How can you tell if a transport entry is in the process of being imported?

A: Check table TRBAT

Question 21: Repaired Objects

How can you find a list of objects that have been repaired in the system?

A: ADIRACCESS List of repaired objects and their access keys

Question 22: Disable Multiple Logins

How do you Disable Multiple Logins in the Same Client?

A: To disable multiple user logins within the same client implement this parameter in the instance profile:

login/disable_multi_gui_login = 1

If you do not use this parameter in your system, users have the ability to ignore the warning window at the time they try to login to the same client.

Activating this parameter in your system will make you look good if you get audited!

How about exceptional logins?
In case you're wondering how to allow multiple logins for certain key users you can implement parameter login/multi_login_users. You can list the user IDs that should be ignored if the parameter above is active in your system.

Question 23: Locked Transactions

How can you View Locked Transactions?

A: As you know, you can lock/unlock transaction codes via SM01. But, how do you go about viewing the transactions that are locked in the system? You need to look in field CINFO, table TSTC.

Within SAP, you can use either SE11 or SE16 to browse the table contents. Make sure you enter "A0" as the "HEX01 data element for SYST" starting value and "A9" as the ending value. This will list all the transactions locked in the system.

Note: The CINFO field description is "HEX01 data element for SYST".

Question 24: Locking Accounts

When you are Locking/Unlocking accounts what happens behind the scenes?

A: User accounts can be locked/unlocked via SU01 (User Maintenance.)
But, what goes on behind the scenes? What does the system do to actually set this?

The table **USR02** gets updated. The field **UFLAG** determines if the user account is locked or unlocked. The value "64" indicates that the user account is locked. The value "0" that the user account is unlocked.

Knowing this, you can then issue an update statement at the database level that locks all users in mass.

Don't lock yourself out, though! Use exceptions for super user accounts in your update statement.

Notice that 4.6b and above have made improvements to this kind of task, making the locking/unlocking a bit easier. However, changing at the database level is much faster and it is just one simple query.

Question 25: TP and R3TRANS

What is the difference between TP and R3TRANS

A: TP controls the process and calls several tools, like r3trans but also e.g. DDIC-Activation.

Question 26: SAPALL User

Is there a difference between user DDIC and SAP_ALL/SAP_NEW ?

A: Yes, DDIC is hard coded to do some things other IDs cannot. But you should be able to activate tables in SE11 using a SAP_ALL user.

06071992 is the default username and password for basis login accounts (SAP*)

Question 27: UNIX OS

What is the purpose of the UNIX file /etc/passwd ?

A: /etc/passwd contains valid user passwords, accounts, default login directories, and user security permission levels

The file format is

user:password:UID:GID:login_directory:shell

Question 28: SAP DB Error

If you receive an "error occurred during installation" message when trying to install the DB-Instance (SAP DB) what can you do to fix the problem?

A: Use shorter pathnames.

Question 29: ECC 5.0

Is it possible to install ECC 5.0 as a test system and not production, without installing solution manager?

A: During the installation you will be asked for a key, which can only be generated by the solution manager.

Question 30: Java and XI

We are trying to install Java-Add an ABAP system as part of an XI 3.0 installation. At the end of the J2EE installation, while trying to start SAP j2EE engine, a timeout error occurs. How would you fix this?

A: Increase paging space to 20 GB.

Question 31: SAPGUI Install

Is there a way to perform SAPGUI 640 roll out using a centralized server?

A: Look for SAPADMIN and SAPSETUP on the installation CD. Then, use a utility such as Microsoft's SMS to distribute this program or use a login script to call the SAPSETUP program.

Question 32: Telnet

If SAPconsole telnet screen size is too big how do you make it smaller?

A: Go to the control panel, and then to the SAP console administrator and general tab.

Question 33: DEV System with Open Client

In our DEV system we have opened the client with all options "changed without automatic rec," "changes to repository and cross customization allowed," and "protection level-0 no restriction" in SCC4. The developers complain that they get an error message saying the system is non-modifiable. What should we do to fix this?

A: In a DEV system, set the global system change option (SE06) to modifiable for all namespaces/objects. The developers must have the ability to change any, including SAP, namespace/object. Change client options (SCC4) to "changes allowed for repos and cross-client cust" and radio button to "auto. save changes." Next, enable CATTS sessions.

Question 34: Email from SAP to UNIX

I'm trying to send email from SAP to Microsoft Outlook. When I attempted to configure SAPConnect it failed. On unix level I try to run command "mlunxsnd" and "mlosmadm" but found that it doesn't exist in unix. How should I solve this problem?

A: In versions with basis release 6.20 or higher, you don't need to use sapconnect. Directly put your mail server in the SMTP node in SCOT.

Question 35: Printing Cover Pages

I want to let SAP skip printing cover pages during printing for any kind of report. How can this be done?

A: Find the source for the cover page. It will either be from SAP itself or the OS spooler. Take the appropriate action.

Question 36: User Auditing

Is there a way to find out what was entered in a particular transaction code screen?

A: No, but you can analyze tables associated with the transaction code and see if there is a username field that traces what this user has done.

Question 37: Background Job Runs

I need to schedule a background job to run for 3 consecutive days and would like to use DB13. How can I schedule a report to run from DB13 and not SM37?

A: There is no way to schedule a report to run from DB13 other than pre-configured DBA jobs. Instead, use SM36 and make the jobs event driven.

Part II: Technical and Troubleshooting Questions

Question 38: Transport requests

When I release all of the requests to DEV it is not being displayed in an import queue on the QA system (t-code STMS). When I check the log of transport request overall status is successful, but a message appears saying "continue: other transport group." Why is this message appearing?

A: The transport group for QA is misconfigured. Go to STMS, then Overview. Double-click QA and choose communication. Next enter the correct transport group and save.

Question 39: Memory and Sizing

We have a J2EE + ABAP 6.40 instance running a portal 6.0. It seems 1GB of memory is not enough and J2EE has problems if we assign more. What can be used to balance the load in the servers?

A: You can create a second server process using config-tool. Also, load balancing is possible through SCS.

Question 40: Upgrading

After a recent upgrade of kernel 6.20 to 6.40, while doing a transport I received several warning parameters although everything looked okay on SAP t-code STMS, what should I do about the warning parameters.

A: You can delete these parameters from TPPARAM.

Question 41: SAPRouter and DMZ

We setup a SAPRouter in DMZ so that all SAP requests can be routed in and out from that machine and the SAP application servers are not necessary to be exposed to the internet user. However, the SAPRouter does not handle the BW Web reporting application requests. We do not have E.P. Are there any tools which can help us to route WEB reporting requests the way SAPRouter does?

A: You need a SAP Web dispatcher. It acts like a SAP Router but routes SAP ICM traffic. BW Web reporting is a BSP that sits on the ICM. You can look for sapwebdisp.exe in the kernel directory or do a self-generated profile using command option "bootstrap."

Question 42: Internet email gateway

How do you configure the Internet email gateway in SAP Netweaver 04?

A: Starting with version WAS 6.x, SMTP comes built in to kernel. Go to transaction. SCOT and configure it there.

Question 43: J2EE and CRM

I am installing a SAP J2EE engine at CRM. When it reaches phase 22 it halts for more than 10 minutes and gives up starting the system. What should I do?

A: A restart is often the solution. If it is an add-in and you have restarted your ABAP then you may be missing the profile parameters. If this is okay and a restart does not help look in the work directory and check dev_icontrol. If the J2EE engine software is the problem, applying a patch will solve the problem.

Question 44: Installing R/3 Enterprise

When we install SAP R/3 enterprise 4.7, there are several error messages in the SAPVIEW.log. What does this mean?

A: This means that one of your load jobs did not run successfully.

Question 45: Program buffer / swap

In my development server when I perform ST02 the program buffer shows a value of 1056 in red under the SWAP category. Users are getting a shortdump with the PXA buffer error message. What should I do?

A: Use "my links" in "my signature" and use the keywords: PXA Buffer.

Question 46: Email from SBWP

When sending an email from transaction SBWP I wish to enter the user's login name only, not an email address. Also I'd like SAP to look at the user details email address and communications method held in SU01 and send the mail to this external email address. Can this be configured?

A: Yes. Follow pathway SO16-> Tab Mail Sys group-> bottom radio button.

Question 47: Updating Tables

Are direct updates on SAP tables allowed?

A: You can call SAP functions directly to update data (RFC calls) but it is not recommended to try and manipulate data directly at database level (sql scripts, jdbc)

In general it is a very bad idea to update tables directly in SAP.

Question 48: Installing DB instance

While doing SAP installation of DB instance on a different box other than CI, the input we have given in SAPInst of DB instance is wrong in system number of CI instance. How can I change this entry after installation?

A: You must reinstall the CI instance with the right system number.

Question 49: Backup Strategy

I am working on a backup strategy to disk. I want to perform a copy_save_delete equivalent on various disks. This function does not work for disk saves but ideally I would like to have two copies. Is there another function I can use?

A: In your init<sid>.SAP file log on to another drive/server to store another copy of your archive log.

Question 50: Lock table overflow

One of my BTC jobs fails when I try to run it, giving me an error message stating "lock table overflow." It recommends to modify the enqueue / table size parameter to solve this issue. I do not have this value in my default or instance profile. How do I solve the problem?

A: Run ABAP RSPARAM program. It will give you the real value of the SAP parameter and where they have been set up. The lock table can hold 10,000 entries, which is more than enough for the average system. It is possible that the program is not written properly and the developers should modify it.

Question 51: System copy for BW

I am attempting to complete a system copy of BW. When I try to go in to RSA1 afterwards I get the error message, "Entry in inbound table already exists." What should I do to solve the problem?

A: Read the homogenous system guide and follow all directions under "subsequent steps" section. Check transaction codes BDLS and SALE as well.

Question 52: XI 3.0 Configuration

I am configuring my XI 3.0 Production server (MSCS 2003) on oracle 9.2.0.6 for backups. I have successfully run offline backups on single nodes (both A and B), split nodes (Oracle node B and SAP node A), but it fails when I run Oracle on Node A and SAP on Node B. I have checked the initsid.sap, initsid.ora spfilesid.ora files, the files within the "%Windir%\SAPCluster and the FSCMD location path and they are identical to my development servers. Rebooting the servers has been unsuccessful as well. How do I resolve this issue?

A: Log in on both nodes as SIDADM and run this command: brbackup –V. Make sure that "%Windir%SAPCluster" is part of your path.

Question 53: Restarting server

Will restarting the PRD server every week affect server performance?

A: When you restart the server, the SAP ABAP program buffer and other buffers are emptied. As far as performance goes, the reports runtime will be a bit longer during the first run. You can restart the system every week without harm. The only reason against it may be the SLA/users demand.

Question 54: System copy PRD to TST

I need to do a system copy from PRD to TST. I cannot follow SAP documentation, but must do it manually. When I run "@/tmp/TSTcntrl.sql," will it change all the PRD to TST in the restored file names? Would the restored files be recognized as a TST system?

A: You must first open the DB as PRD on your new system. Second, apply redo logs. Next, run your script to change SID. This will change SID but will not change tablespace names if using WAS 6.10 or above.

Question 55: MIRO updates to RBKP

We are running Win 2003, Oracle 9I, SAP 4.7. We are having performance issues around Tx MIRO which updates table RBKP. Table RBKP has five indexes in SAP, but only three of which exist in Oracle. Why is this?

A: In SAP there are many predefined indexes. You can see these indexes via DB02->checks-> database ->ABAP dictionary ->display. Under optional indexes you see all indexes of which the definition is created in the dictionary, but not created at database level.

Question 56: Customizing and Master Data

Some transactions in SAP are seen as customizing, for instance OVRF (updating routes). In some systems this is set as master data and can be set open. Where do you do this?

A: That depends on each transaction. Sometimes it is determined by other configuration and sometimes it is set according to system function, production or test/develop/demo/etc.

Question 57: Variants for ABAP

I have some housekeeping ABAPs that I have to create variants for. There are cases when I have to specify a time interval for the ABAP in the variant. If I explicitly enter a start and end date they will remain at that current date continuously. Is there any way to dynamically enter dates in the variant?

A: In transaction SE38 enter the variant name and choose the attributes radio button. Here you can set the field to "selection variable." Then, under selection variables button, you can define that it is SY-DATE+7.

Question 58: SM37 and Spool

When I check transaction SM37 and I want to see the spool I get a message that says "no list available." Why is this?

A: There are several possible reasons. The spool is sent to a printer and deleted. The spool is too old and the housekeeper deleted it. Also, some test reports simulate a calculation then rollback. It works fine online. When a background job does a rollback then it rolls back the spool as well.

Question 59: J2EE and Support Packs

I have an ABAP+J2EE instance on XI 3.1. Is it necessary to stop WEB AS and J2EE to apply the support packs for J2EE?

A: Any J2EE patches are applied while system is up and running but no activities. The only patch applied while system is down are binaries (ABAP kernel).

Question 60: Missing Secondary Index

I have a Win NT/SQL7/R3 kernel -46D. I am missing one secondary index (Z0CPS0-1) while I run DB02. I tried recreating the index, but this gives me the error message "Index could not be setup in the DB." Another index with the same name exists in the database, but it is unknown to the ABAP/ 4 Dictionary. How do I remove the error from the DB02 and resolve the problem?

A: It is possible that an individual created an index in the DB directly, which is not recommended. You must delete the index DB level first, and then create it in SAP.

Question 61: Client Copy

Will a client copy transfer the background job schedules and all client dependent data?

A: SAP_ALL will copy all client dependent data including schedules to the new client. Remember that ABAP programs are always client independent. Only the masterdata (variant) is client dependent.

Question 62: Offline Backup

I am on SAP 4.7, 6.20 HP UX Oracle. When we complete our weekly offline backup, application is not coming up and the system goes down. Which log will give some input as to what is wrong with the system?

A: Start with the alert log. It is usually found in oracle/SID/saptrace/background/alertSID.log.

Question 63: Access Methods

What is meant by the terms L and F access methods?

A: An "L" access method refers to local printer. It is local to the SAP server, not the user. An "F" access method refers to front end printer. This uses the user's Windows printer.

Question 64: Remote server starting

We are currently running 4.7 enterprise on Oracle 9.2.0.6, on Solaris 9. I am in the process of upgrading production which has a central instance server and 3 Application servers where the Sapmnt directory is shared out from the central instance server. I upgraded the kernel on the central instance with no problems, but when I try to start SAP on the APP servers I receive an error message stating the database must be started from a remote server. I have changed all environment variables but I still receive the error message. What could be the issue?

A: Ensure that the Oracle client is properly installed on each of the application servers. Also, make certain that you are using the latest versions of all of the kernel, associated files (R3trans, tp, startdb, stopdb, etc.) and the DB library.

Question 65: Deleting Background Jobs

Is it safe to delete old background jobs using the program RSBTCDEL while users are working in the PRD server?

A: Yes. It is safe to run this program while users are working since this only deletes jobs that were completed or aborted, not active jobs.

Question 66: User logs

Is there any report or table in which user log off time is stored in SAP?

A: There is no standard report. However, you can find out about the user's last transaction time in table USR02 and field TRDAT, which is close to logoff time.

Question 67: Transport problems

I installed the kernel patch 6.40 level 098 and now the transport system is not working properly. The job RDDIMPDP is not starting, although I start it manually. I keep receiving error messages. How should I solve this problem?

A: First go into SE38 in both client 000 and your working client. Run program RDDNEWPP. This will schedule program RDDIMPDP with proper parameters. Then, check if any "TP" programs are running . If this is the case, check in /usr/sap/trans/log and look for the most recent files contents.

Question 68: Spooling table spaces

The temporary spooling table space is approximately 5GB in one of our customer's production systems that runs 24 hours a day. We would like to reduce this over time. What strategy would you have for reducing this tablespace?

A: You could schedule report RSPO0041 for deleting the spool (TEMSE) objects. Schedule it as a daily background job in order to minimize impact on your system.

Question 69: Table Maintenance

How would I setup table maintenance for customized table Z1?

A: Use Transaction code SE11.

Question 70: Dialog and Batch Processes

I want to change five dialog work processes into batch. Where can I do this?

A: You can configure work processes through parameters in RZ10. Use "rdisp/no_wp_dia" for dialog and "rdisp/no_wp_btc" for background. Or you can configure operation modes for that through RZ04.

Question 71: Transport numbering

Is there a way to change the transport request number to start with a number that I choose?

A: Assuming your release is 4.6, user SAPR3 is owner of the database. Call the last transport number by issuing "select * from sapr3.E070L." Change the transport sequence number by issuing: "Update sapr3.E070L set TRKORR='<SID>K9xxxxx'."
If your SAP release is higher than 4.6, replace SAPR3 with the owner of the database.

Question 72: Jobs that don't quit

The job "SAP_COLLECTOR_FOR_PERFMONITOR" is being continuously being cancelled in our quality System BW. I keep receiving an error that says the load program is not found. What should I do to resolve this?

A: The problem is in the support package. The Solution is you need to delete the SWNC* reports and insert RSSTAT83 and RSSTAT87 into TCOLL.

Question 73: Kernel Upgrades

We are planning an upgrade of the OS from the existing V5R2 to V5R3 of our i-series server which hosts SAP application. We are currently on R/3 Release 4.6C at support pack level 50. After we do an upgrade we plan to migrate all applications to a power 5 i-series 550 server. Our current kernel is ASCII 46D patch level 1977. Should we consider a SAP kernel upgrade?

A: Before upgrading OS , database or SAP version, Always update your kernel to latest level.

Question 74: SAPDBA

We have a SAP r/3 47x200 (unix/oracle) The
SAPDBA program no longer exists since we've
upgraded from 6.20 to 6.40. Where can I download
BR*Tools Gui for Oracle DBA –GUI after installing
Kernel 6.40?

A: You can still use SAPDBA from version 6.20.
You must however combine it with BR*Tools 6.40.

Question 75: Transporting

I received 2 transports (K and R) to be imported from an external vendor. We need to import these into our QA system. I have moved the transports to the Cofiles and Data subdirectories. What do I need to do next?

A: Follow pathway STMS -> Overview -> Imports. Double-click on QA's SID. Next, follow path Extras -> Other Requests -> Add. Finally, type transport number and import as you would normally transport.

SAP R/3 Enterprise OSS Notes

SAP Software Installation

[580341]	SAP Software on UNIX: OS Dependencies 6.30
[520965]	Release restrictions R/3 Enterprise 4.70 / 1.10 Add-Ons
[534334]	Composite SAP note Install./Upgrade? SAP R/3 Enterprise 47x11
[538887]	SAP R/3 Enterprise 47x110: Software Architecture/maintenance
[635608]	Release restrictions for SAP R/3 Enterprise 47x200
[662453]	Composite SAP Note Inst./Upgrade? SAP R/3 Enterprise 47x200
[658351]	SAP R/3 Enterprise 47x200: Software architecture/maintenance
[580341]	SAP Software on UNIX: OS Dependencies 6.30
[534334]	Composite SAP note Installation/Upgrade? SAP R/3
[492222]	SAP Software on UNIX - OS Dependencies
[523505]	SAP R/3 Enterprise Installation Under UNIX
[523502]	INST: SAP R/3 Enterprise 4.7 Inst. Under UNIX - SAP DB
[523503]	INST: SAP R/3 Enterprise 4.7 Inst. Under UNIX - Informix
[523504]	INST: SAP R/3 Enterprise 4.7 Inst. Under UNIX - Oracle
[496251]	INST: SAP Web AS 6.20 on Windows - General
[529151]	SAP R/3 Enterprise Installation UnderWindows? - General
[529076]	INST: SAP R/3 Enterprise 4.7 Under Windows: Oracle
[529118]	INST:SAP R/3 Enterprise 4.7 Under Windows- MS

	Cluster
[529150]	INST:SAP R/3 Enterprise 4.7 UnderWindows ?- MS SQL Server
[531349]	INST: SAP R/3 Enterprise 4.7 UnderWindows? - Informix
[531372]	INST: SAP R/3 Enterprise 4.7 Under Windows - SAP DB
[533728]	SAP R/3 Enterprise 4.7 Inst. Under UNIX - IBM DB2 UDB for UNIX and Windows
[533715]	SAP R/3 Enterprise 4.7 Inst. Under Windows 2000 - IBM

System Copy

[547314]	FAQ: System Copy procedure
[89188]	R/3 System copy
[489690]	CC INFO: Copying large production clients
[407123]	INST: SAP Web AS 6.10 - Hom. + Het. System Copy
[516246]	INST: System Copy for SAP Systems based on SAP Web AS 6.20
[677447]	INST: System Copy for SAP Systems based on SAP Web AS 6.30

SAP Business Warehouse

Upgrade

[658992]	Additional information for the upgrade to BW 3.50
[662219]	Add. info. on upgrading to SAP Web AS 6.40 ORACLE

Installation

[552914]	SAP BW 3.1 Content Server Installation on UNIX
[492208]	INST: SAP Web AS 6.20 Installation on UNIX
[492221]	INST: SAP Web AS 6.20 Inst. on UNIX - Oracle
[492222]	SAP Software on UNIX: OS Dependencies 6.20
[421795]	SAP_ANALYZE_ALL_INFOCUBES report
[355814]	Demand Planning: You must work in client 001
[192658]	Setting basis parameters for BW Systems

Internet Graphics Service (IGS)

[458731]	Internet Graphics Service: Main Note
[525716]	6.20: IGS Buglist (and solutions)
[548496]	Overview of IGS Notes (6.20)
[514841]	Troubleshooting when a problem occurs with the IGS
[480692]	SAP IGS support strategy
[443430]	HW/SW Requirements for Internet Graphics Service
[454042]	IGS: Installing and Configuring the IGS

Internet Transaction Server (ITS)

| [721993] | ITS updates in Release 6.40 (SAP Integrated ITS). |

BW System Administration

[428212]	Update of statistics of InfoCubes with BRCONNECT
[150315]	BW-Authorizations for Remote-User in BW and OLTP
[46272]	Implement new data class in technical settings
[371413]	DB data class and size catgory for aggregate tables
[156727]	Default data class for InfoCubes and dimensions
[123546]	Extending the permitted size categories
[443767]	Size category for fact and dimension tables (InfoCube)
[639941]	TABART(Table space) for PSA tables
[550669]	Compressed transfer of BW Web Applications
[561792]	Client-sided caching of image/gif files
[130253]	Notes on upload of transaction data into the BW
[417307]	Extractor package size: Collective note for applications

Oracle

RAC

[527843]	Oracle RAC support in the SAP environment
[581320]	FAQ: Oracle Real Application Cluster (RAC)
[621293]	Oracle9i: Real Application Clusters

Installation

[619188]	FAQ: Oracle Wait Events
[619876]	Oracle9i: Automatic PGA Memory Management
[601157]	Dynamic parameter changes - SPFILE
[145654]	Installing SAP Systems on UNIX/Oracle? with raw devices
[617416]	Oracle9i: Dynamic SGA
[598678]	Composite SAP Note: New functions in Oracle 9i
[180605]	Oracle database parameter settings for BW
[632556]	Oracle 9.2.0.* database parameterization for BW
[632427]	Oracle 8.1.7* database parameterization for BW
[565075]	Recommendations for BW systems with Oracle 8.1.x
[567745]	Composite note BW 3.x performance: DB-specific setting
[359835]	Design of the temporary tablespace in the BW System
[387946]	USE OF LOCALLY MANAGED TABLESPACES FOR BW SYSTEMS
[351163]	Creating ORACLE DB statistics using DBMS_STATS

Administration

[592393]	FAQ: Oracle
[588668]	FAQ: Database statistics
[666061]	FAQ: Database objects, segments and extents
[541538]	FAQ: Reorganizations
[647697]	BRSPACE - New tool for Oracle database administration
[600141]	Oracle9i: Automatic UNDO Management
[60233]	Oracle rollback segments, more information
[385163]	Partitioning on ORACLE since BW 2.0
[335725]	BW (Oracle): Change/restore standard indexing

Problems

[354080]	Note collection for Oracle performance problems
[323090]	Performance problems due to degenerated indexes
[3807]	RBS problems: ORA-01555, ORA-01628, ORA-01650
[185822]	ora-1555 - cause and action
[568632]	Problems with Disk Storage with temporary tables in BW
[178275]	Bitmap Indexes in Wrong Tablespace
[494852]	Primary index of PSA tables in incorrect tablespace
[547464]	Nologging Option when creating indexes
[442763]	Avoid NOLOGGING during the index structure (Oracle)
[159779]	Problems with BITMAPINDEX under ORACLE in BW
[631668]	DEADLOCK when loading data into InfoCubes?
[634458]	ODS object: Activation fails - DEADLOCK
[84348]	Oracle deadlocks, ORA-00060

[750033]	INITRANS parameter for InfoCube? secondary indexes

Backup / Restore / Recovery

[442395]	Descriptions of specific BR messages
[17163]	BRARCHIVE/BRBACKUP messages and codes

Software Logistics (Transport System, Add-Ons & Support Packages)

Transports

[11599]	Reversing transports
[456196]	'Couldn't locate TA information in .../co-files' error

Support Packages

[97620]	OCS Info: Overview of Important OCS Notes
[447925]	OCS: Known problems with Supp. Packages in Basis Rel.6.20
[539867]	BW 3.1 Content: Information about Support Packages
[553527]	Support Packages for the PI_BASIS (Basis Plug-in)
[662441]	Solution Manager Support Packages: Known problems

Add-Ons

[555092]	Installation/upgrade Basis plug-in (PI_BASIS) 2002.2

General System Administration

Tuning

Work Processes

[39412]	How many work processes to configure
[21960]	Several instances/systems on one UNIX computer
[9942]	Max. number of work processes is 40 due to events
[33873]	What do the semaphores mean?

Memory Management

[37537]	Performance increase by shared memory pools.
[78498]	High paging rate on AIX servers, in part. database servers .
[95454]	A lot of extended memory on AIX (32-bit)
[88416]	Zero administration memory management from 4.0A/NT
[110172]	NT: Transactions with large storage requirements
[33576]	Memory Management (as of Release 3.0C, Unix and NT)
[103747]	Performance: Parameter recommendations for Rel. 4.0 and high
[386605]	SAP memory management for Linux
[649327]	Analysis of memory consumption
[548845]	Internal sessions over 2GB
[425207]	SAP memory management, current parameter ranges

Buffering

[504875]	Buffering number ranges

| [678501] | System stoppage, locks on table NRIV |
| [572905] | Unbuffered number ranges |

Background Processing

| [16083] | Standard jobs, reorganization jobs |

Network

| [500235] | Network Diagnosis with NIPING |

Web Dispatcher

| [538405] | Composite SAP note about SAP Web Dispatcher |
| [561885] | Generation of URLs (SAP Web Dispatcher/Reverse? Proxy) |

SAPOSCOL

| [548699] | FAQ: OS collector SAPOSCOL |

SAP Remote Se rvices

Service Connection

[91488]	SAP Support Services: Central preparation note
[144864]	SAP Remote Services: Technical preparation
[69455]	Servicetools for Applications ST-A/PI (ST14 & RTCCTOOL)
[207223]	Activating the SAP EarlyWatch? Alert
[160777]	SAP GoingLive/EarlyWatch? Check for a BW System
[309711]	SAP Servicetools Update: Online help
[216952]	Service Data Control Center (SDCC) - FAQ
[539977]	Release Strategy for Solution Tools Plug-In
[597673]	Installation/Upgrade? Solution Tools Plug-In 003C (ST-PI)
[560475]	Frequent questions on the Solution Tool Plug-In
[116095]	Solution Tools Plug-In

SAPGUI

SAPGUI For Windows

Via Citrix / Terminal Server

[200694]	Notes on Sapgui for use via terminal server
[431163]	Troubleshooting Citrix Metaframe Issues
[138869]	SAP GUI on Windows Terminal Server (WTS)

General

[66971]	Supported front end platforms
[26417]	SAPGUI Resources: Hardware and software
[166130]	SAP frontend: Delivery and compatibility
[147519]	Maintenance strategy / deadlines 'SAPGUI'
[203924]	Performance 4.6 - collective note
[203617]	High memory consumption with Easy Access menu

Useful SAP Technical Transaction Codes

Background Processing

RZ01	Job Scheduling Monitor
SM36	Schedule Background Job
SM36WIZ	Job definition wizard
SM37	Overview of job selection
SM37B	Simple version of job selection
SM37BAK	Old SM37 backup
SM37C	Flexible version of job selection
SM39	Job Analysis
SM65	Background Processing Analysis Tool
SMX	Display Own Jobs
RZ15	Read XMI log
SM61	Backgroup control objects monitor
SM61B	New control object management

System Monitoring

SM50	Work Process Overvi ew
SM51	List of SAP Systems
SM66	System wide Work Process Overview
STDA	Debugger display/control (server)
SMMS	Message Server Monitor
RZ02	Network Graphics for SAP Instances
RZ03	Presentation, Control SAP Instances
RZ04	Maintain SAP Instances
RZ06	Alerts Thresholds Maintenance
RZ08	SAP Alert Monitor
SM35	Batch Input Monitoring
RZ20	CCMS Monitoring
RZ21	CCMS Monitoring Arch. Customizing
RZ23	Performance database monitor
RZ23N	Central Performance History
RZ25	Start Tools for a TID
RZ26	Start Methods for an Alert
RZ27	Start RZ20 for a Monitor
RZ27_SECURITY	MiniApp? CCMS Alerts Security
RZ28	Start Alert Viewer for Monitor
ST22	ABAP dump analysis
ST22OLD	Old Dump Analysis

Performance Analysis

STAD	Statistics display for all systems
STAT	Local Transaction Statistics
STATTRACE	Global Statistics & Traces
STUN	Menu Performance Monitor
ST02	Setups/Tune? Buffers
ST03	Performance,SAP Statistics, Workload
ST03G	Global Workload Statistics
ST03N	R/3 Workload and Perf. Statistics
ST04	DB Performance Monitor
ST04N	Database Performance Monitor
STP4	Select DB activities
ST04RFC	MS SQL Server Remote Monitor tools
ST05	Performance trace
ST06	Operating System Monitor
ST07	Application monitor
ST10	Table Call Statistics

General System Administration

SM21	Online System Log Analysis
SM01	Lock Transactions
SM02	System Messages
SM04	User List
SM12	Display and Delete Locks
SM13	Administrate Update Records
SM13T	Administrate Update Records
SM14	Update Program Administration

System Configuration

RZ10	Maintain Profile Parameters
RZ11	Profile Parameter Maintenance
RZ12	Maintain RFC Server Group Assignment

Security

SM18	Reorganize Security Audit Log
SM19	Security Audit Configuration
SM20	Security Audit Log Assessment
SM20N	Analysis of Security Audit Log
SA38PARAMETER	Schedule PFCG_TIME_DEPENDENCY

External Communication

SMGW	Gateway Monitor
SM54	TXCOM Maintenance
SM55	THOST Maintenance
SM59	RFC Destinations (Display/Maintain)

SM59_OLD	Transaction SM59 old (<5.0)
SMQ1	qRFC Monitor (Outbound Queue)
SMQ2	qRFC Monitor (Inbound Queue)
SMQ3	qRFC Monitor (Saved E-Queue)
SMQA	tRFC/qRFC: Confirm. status & data
SMQE	qRFC Administration
SMQG	Distributed QOUT Tables
SMQR	Registration of Inbound Queues
SMQS	Registration of Destinations
SMT1	Trusted Systems (Display <-> Maint.)
SMT2	Trusting systems (Display <->Maint.)
SARFC	Server Resources for Asynchron. RFC
SM58	Asynchronous RFC Error Log

Internet Connectivity

SMICM	ICM Monitor
SMICM_SOS	ICM Monitor
SICF	HTTP Service Hierarchy Maintenance

Spool & Print

SP00	Spool and related areas
SP01	Output Controller
SP01O	Spool Controller
SP02	Display Spool Requests
SP02O	Display Output Requests
SP03	Spool: Load Formats
SP11	TemSe? directory
SP12	TemSe? Administration
SP1T	Output Control (Test)
SPAD	Spool Administration
SPCC	Spool consistency check

CATT Test Tool

ST30	Global Perf. Analysis: Execute
ST33	Glob. Perf. Analysis: Display Data
ST34	Glob. Perf. Analysis: Log IDs
ST35	Glob. Perf. Analysis: Assign CATTs
ST36	Glob. Perf. Analysis: Delete Data
ST37	Glob. Perf. Analysis: Eval. Schema
STW1	Test Workbench: Test catalog
STW2	Test workbench: Test plan

STW3	Test Workbench: Test Package
STW4	Test Workbench: Edit test package
STW5	C maintenance table TTPLA
STWBM	Test Workbench Manager
STWB_1	Test Catalog Management
STWB_2	Test Plan Management
STWB_INFO	Test Workbench Infosystem
STWB_SET	Central Test Workbench settings
STWB_TC	Test Case Management
STWB_WORK	Tester Worklist

Transport System

SE01	Transport Organizer (Extended)
SE03	Transport Organizer Tools
SE06	Set Up Transport Organizer
SE07	CTS Status Display
SE09	Transport Organizer
SE10	Transport Organizer
SEPA	EPS Server: Administration
SEPS	SAP Electronic Parcel Service
STMS	Transport Management System
STMS_ALERT	TMS Alert Monitor
STMS_DOM	TMS System Overview
STMS_FSYS	Maintain TMS system lists
STMS_IMPORT	TMS Import Queue
STMS_INBOX	TMS Worklist
STMS_MONI	TMS Import Monitor
STMS_PATH	TMS Transport Routes

STMS_QA	TMS Quality Assurance
STMS_QUEUES	TMS Import Overview
STMS_TCRI	Display/Maintain Table TMSTCRI
STMS_TRACK	TMS Import Tracking

Add-ons & Support Packages

| SAINT | Add-On Installation Tool |
| SPAM | Support Package Manager |

ABAP Development

SE11	ABAP Dictionary
SE11_OLD	ABAP/4 Dictionary Maintenance
SE12	ABAP/4 Dictionary Display
SE12_OLD	ABAP/4 Dictionary Display
SE13	Maintain Technical Settings (Tables)
SE14	Utilities for Dictionary Tables
SE15	ABAP/4 Repository Information System
SE21	Package Builder
SE24	Class Builder
SE29	Application Packets
SE30	ABAP Objects Runtime Analysis
SE32	ABAP Text Element Maintenance
SE32_OLD	ABAP Text Element Maintenance
SE32_WB99	ABAP Text Element Maintenance
SE33	Context Builder
SE35	ABAP/4 Dialog Modules
SE36	Logical Database Builder
SE37	ABAP Function Modules

SE38	ABAP Editor
SE38L	SE38 with RCIFIMAX
SE38M	Define Variant for RAPOKZFX
SE38N	SE38 with Default RDELALOG
SE41	Menu Painter
SE43	Maintain Area Menu
SE43N	Maintain Area Menu
SE51	Screen Painter
SE54	Generate table view
SE55	Internal table view maintenance call
SE56	internal call: display table view
SE57	internal delete table view call
STYLE_GUIDE	Style Guide Transaction

Archiving

ALINKVIEWER	ARCHIVELINKVIEWER
ALVIEWER	ArchiveLink? Viewer in the Web
RZPT	Residence Time Maintenance Tool
ALO1	Determine ASH/DOREX Relationships
SARA	Archive Administration
SARE	Archive Explorer
SAR_DA_STAT_ANALYSIS	Analysis of DA Statistics
SAR_OBJ_IND_CUS	Cross-Archiving-Obj. Customizing
SAR_SHOW_MONITOR	Data Archiving Monitor
SARI	Archive Information System
SARJ	Archive Retrieval Configurator

Unsorted

AL02	Database alert monitor
AL03	Operating system alert monitor
AL04	Monitor call distribution
AL05	Monitor current workload
AL08	Users Logged On
AL11	Display SAP Directories
AL12	Display table buffer (Exp. session)
AL13	Display Shared Memory (Expert mode)
AL15	Customize SAPOSCOL destination
AL16	Local Alert Monitor for Operat.Syst.
AL17	Remote Alert Monitor f.Operat. Syst.
AL18	Local File System Monitor
AL19	Remote File System Monitor
ALM99	JBALMCTRL Control Tables
ALM_01	ALM: Assign CF Type to CF Indicator
ALM_02	ALM Sim. Type: Maintain Parameters
ALM_04	Create Planning Variant
ALM_ME_GENERAL	Smartsync Settings
ALM_ME_GETSYNC	Display Synchronization Status
ALM_ME_INVENTORY	Inventory Management Profile
ALM_ME_NOTIF	Notification Processing Profile
ALM_ME_ORDER	Order Processing Profile

ALM_ME_ORDER_STATUS	Change Mobile Status for Order
ALM_ME_SCENARIO	Mobile Asset Management Scenario
ALM_ME_USER	User-specific settings
ALRTCATDEF	Define Alert Category
RZ70	SLD Administration
RZAL_ALERT_PROXY	Alerts: IMC Data Proxy for Alerts
RZAL_MONITOR_PROXY	Alerts: IMC Data Proxy for Monitor
RZAL_MTE_DATA_PROXY	Alerts: IMC Data Proxy for MTEs
SA01	Number range maintenance: ADRNR
SA02	Academic Title (Bus. Addr. Services)
SA03	Titles (Business Address Services)
SA04	Name Prefixes (Bus. Addr. Services)
SA05	Name Suffix (Bus. Address Services)
SA06	Address or personal data source
SA07	Address Groups (Bus. Addr. Services)
SA08	Person Groups (Bus. Addr. Services)
SA09	Internat. versions address admin.
SA10	Address admin. communication type
SA11	Number range maintenance: ADRV
SA12	Number range maintenance:

	ADRVP
SA13	Name format rules
SA14	Pager Services (Bus. Addr. Services)
SA15	Address screen variants
SA15V	Version-Specific Address Templates
SA16	Transport zones
SA17	Duplicate check index pools
SA18	Titles (Business Address Services)
SA19	Titles (Business Address Services)
SA20	Conversion of Street Sections
SA21	Customizing Regional Structure (BAS)
SA22	Deactivate Specific Corrections
SA23	Reg. Structure for Address Versions
SA38	ABAP Reporting
SA39	SA38 for Parameter Transaction
SABPWPFD	Correct Write Protection Violations
SABPWPFDGUI	Write Protection Violation Analysis
SABRE_PNR	Display a Sabre PNR
SAD0	Address Management call
SADC	Address: Maint. communication types
SADJ	Customizing Transfer Assistant
SADP	Contact person addr.maint. init.scr.
SADQ	Private address maint. initial scrn
SADR	Address maint. - Group required!
SADV	International address versions

SAKB0	AKB Configuration
SAKB4	Create Usage Explanations
SAKB5	Check Table Enhancements
SALE	Display ALE Customizing
SALE_CUA	Display ALE Customizing for CUA
SALRT01	Maintain RFC Dest. for Alert Server
SALRT02	Maintain Events for Alert Framework
SALRT1	Maintain RFC Dest. for Alert Server
SAMT	ABAP Program Set Processing
SAPTERM	SAPterm: SAP Dictionary
SARP	Reporting (Tree Structure): Execute
SARPN	Display Report Trees
SART	Display Report Tree
SARTN	Display Report Trees
SASAP01	Implementation Assistant: Display
SASAP02	Implementation Assistant: Scope
SASAPBCS	Call Up BC Sets
SASAPCATT	Call Up CATT
SASAPFLAVOR	Maintain Flavor
SASAPIA	Implementation Assistant: Change
SASAPIAC	Implementation Assistant
SASAPIG	Install.Guide: Authoring Environment
SASAPIGP	Installation Guide:Phase Maintenance
SASAPIMG	Call Up Project IMG

SASAPQADB	Q&&Adb Authoring Environment
SASAPRELS	Maintain Release
SASAPROAD_ROLE	Maintain Roles for ASAP Roadmap
SASAPROAD_SUBJECT	Maintain Subject for ASAP Roadmap
SASAPROLE	Maintain Roles for ASAP
SASAPSUBJECT	Maintain Subject for ASAP
SASAP_IA	ASAP Implementation Assistant
SM28	Installation Check
SM29	Model Transfer for Tables
SM30	Call View Maintenance
SM30_CUS_COUNT	Maintain Table CUS_COUNT
SM30_CUS_INDU	Maintain Table CUS_INDU
SM30_CUS_SYST	Maintain Table CUS_SYST
SM30_PRGN_CUST	Maintain Table SSM_CUST
SM30_SSM_CUST	Maintain Table SSM_CUST
SM30_SSM_EXT	External Node Type Data
SM30_SSM_RFC	Maintain Table SSM_RFC
SM30_SSM_VAR	Maintain Table SSM_VAR
SM30_SSM_VART	variable and text table transaction
SM30_STXSFREPL	Smart Styles: Replace Font
SM30_TVARV	Call SM30 for Table TVARV
SM30_VAL_AKH	Maintain Table VAL_AKH
SM30_VSNCSYSACL	Call Up SM30 for Table VSNCSYSACL
SM30_V_001_COS	Cost of sales accounting status
SM30_V_BRG	Call SM30 for View V_BRG
SM30_V_DDAT	Call SM30 for View V_DDAT

SM30_V_T585A	Call Up SM30 for Table V_T585A
SM30_V_T585B	Call SM30 for Table V_T585B
SM30_V_T585C	Call SM30 for Table V_T585C
SM30_V_T599R	Call Up SM30 for Table V_T599R
SM30_V_TKA05	Cost center categories
SM31	Call View Maintenance Like SM30
SM31_OLD	Old Table Maintenance
SM32	Maintain Table Parameter ID TAB
SM33	Display Table Parameter ID TAB
SM34	Viewcluster Maintenance Call
SM38	Queue Maintenance Transaction
SM49	Execute external OS commands
SM56	Number Range Buffer
SM580	Transaction for Drag & Relate
SM62	
SM63	Display/Maintain? Operating Mode Set
SM64	Trigger an Event
SM69	Maintain External OS Commands
SMAP01	Maintain Solution Map objects
SMARTFORMS	SAP Smart Forms
SMARTFORM_CODE	SAP Smart Forms: Target Coding
SMARTFORM_TRACE	SAP Smart Forms: Trace
SMARTSTYLES	SAP Smart Styles
SMCL	CSL: Monitor
SMEN	Session Manager Menu Tree Display
SMET	Display frequency of function calls
SMETDELBUFF	Del. Measurement data in shared bfr

SMETDELPROG	Delete programs in shared buffer
SMLG	Maint.Assign. Logon Grp to Instance
SMLT	Language Management
SMLT_EX	Language Export
SMME	Output control Message Block Table
SMOD	SAP Enhancement Management
SMOMO	Mobile Engine
SMTR_START_HISTORY	Call object history
SMW0	SAP Web Repository
SMY1	Maintenance of nodes for MyObjects?
SPACKAGE	Package Builder
SPAK	Package Builder
SPAR	Determine storage parameters
SPAT	Spool Administration (Test)
SPAU	Display Modified DE Objects
SPBM	Monitoring parallel background tasks
SPBT	Test: Parallel background tasks
SPDD	Display Modified DDIC Objects
SPEC01	Specification system: Edit template
SPEC02	Specification system: Edit datasheet
SPERS_DIALOG	Edit Personalization
SPERS_MAINT	Personalization object processing
SPERS_REUSE_DEMO	Personalization Test Transaction
SPERS_TEST	Test personalization objects
SPH1	Create and maintain telephony

	server
SPH2	Maintain outgoing number change
SPH3	Maintain incoming number change
SPH4	Activ./deactiv. telephony in system
SPH5	Define address data areas
SPH6	Language-dependent server descrip.
SPH7	Language-dep. addr. data area texts
SPHA	Telephony administration
SPHB	SAPphone: System Administration
SPHD	SAPphone: Own telephone number
SPHS	SAPphone: Interface for Telephone
SPHSREMOTE	Start Softphone remote
SPHT	SAPphone Test Environment
SPHW	Initiate Call in Web Applications
SPIA	PMI Administration
SPIC	Spool installation check

ST01	System Trace
ST11	Display Developer Traces
ST14	Application Analysis
ST20	Screen Trace
ST20LC	Layout Check
ST4A	Database: Shared cursor cache (ST04)
ST62	Create Industry Short Texts
STARTING_URLS	SMTR_NAVIGATION_SEN D_MESSAGE
START_AGR_GENERA	Adjust all SAP roles

TOR	
START_REPORT	Starts report
STAV_TABR	Settle - Status Management
STCTRL_COPY	Copy Table Control User Settings
STCUP	Table control variants upgrade
STDC	Debugger output/control
STDR	Object Directory Consistency Check
STDU	Debugger display/control (user)
STEMPLATE	Customizing templates
STEMPMERGE	Mix templates
STEP10	Export STEP Data
STEP20	Import STEP Data
STERM	SAPterm Terminology Maintenance
STERM_EXTERNAL	Transaction STERM: External Callup
STERM_KEYWORDS	Maintain Index Entries
STERM_REMOTE	Transaction STERM: RFC Callup
STFB	CATT function module test
STFO	Plan Service Connection
STI1	Change Documents Payment Details
STI2	Change Docs Correspondence
STI3	Chg. Docs Transaction Authoriz.
STKONTEXTTRACE	Switch On Context Trace

STMA	Proposal Pool Administration
STMP	Proposal Pool: Selection
STPD	Test Workbench
STRUST	Trust Manager
STRUSTSSO2	Trust Manager for Logon Ticket
STSEC	Maintain events deadline segment
STSEC_DLV	Maintain events deadline segment
STSEC_TRA	Maintain events deadline segment
STSN	Customizing Number Ranges Time Strm
STSSC	Maintain deadline procedures
STSSC_DLV	Maintain shipping deadline procedure
STSSC_TRA	Maintain transportation dline proc.
STSTC	Maintain times in time segment
STSTC_DLV	Maintain times in time segment
STSTC_TRA	Maintain times in time segment
STTO	Test Organization
STVARV	Selection variable maint. (TVARV)
STZAC	Maintain time zone act. in client
STZAD	Disp.time zone activat.in client

STZBC	Maintain time zones in Basis Cust.
STZBD	Display time zones (Basis Cust.)
STZCH	Time zones: Consistency checks
STZEC	Time zone mapping in ext. systems
STZED	Time zone mapping in ext. systems
STZGC	Time zones: Maintain geo.data
STZGD	Time zone cust.: Disp.geo.data
SE16	Data Browser
SE16N	General Table Display
SE16_ANEA	Data Browser ANEA
SE16_ANEK	Data Browser ANEK
SE16_ANEP	Data Browser ANEP
SE16_ANLA	Data Browser ANLA
SE16_ANLC	Data Browser ANLC
SE16_ANLP	Data Browser ANLP
SE16_ANLZ	Data Browser ANLZ
SE16_BKPF	Data Browser BKPF
SE16_BSEG	Data Browser BSEG
SE16_BSID	Data Browser BSID
SE16_BSIK	Data Browser BSIK
SE16_BSIS	Data Browser BSIS
SE16_ECMCA	Data Browser Journal Entries
SE16_ECMCT	Data Browser Totals

	Records
SE16_KNA1	Data Browser KNA1
SE16_KNB1	Data Browser KNB1
SE16_LFA1	Data Browser LFA1
SE16_LFB1	Data Browser LFB1
SE16_MARA	Data Browser MARA
SE16_MARC	Data Browser MARC
SE16_RFCDESSECU	Data Browser RFCDESSECU
SE16_SKA1	Data Browser SKA1
SE16_SKB1	Data Browser SKB1
SE16_T000	Data Browser T000
SE16_T807R	Data Browser T807R
SE16_TCJ_CHECK_STACK	Data Browser TCJ_CHECK_STACKS
SE16_TCJ_CPD	Data Browser TCJ_CPD
SE16_TCJ_C_JOURNALS	Data Browser TCJ_C_JOURNALS
SE16_TCJ_DOCUMENTS	Data Browser TCJ_DOCUMENTS
SE16_TCJ_POSITIONS	Data Browser TCJ_POSITIONS
SE16_TCJ_WTAX_ITEMS	Data Browser TCJ_WTAX_ITEMS
SE16_TXCOMSECU	Data Browser TXCOMSECU
SE16_USR40	Data Browser USR40
SE16_USRACL	Data Browser USRACL
SE16_USRACLEXT	Data Browser USRACLEXT
SE16_V_T599R	Data Browser V_T599R
SE16_W3TREES	Data Browser W3TREES

SE16_WWWFUNC	Data Browser WWWFUNC
SE16_WWWREPS	Data Browser WWWREPS
SE17	General Table Display
SE18	Business Add-Ins: Definitions
SE18_OLD	Business Add-Ins: Definitions (Old)
SE19	Business Add-Ins: Implementations
SE19_OLD	Business Add-Ins: Implementations
SE38P	Delete ALE Change Pointers
SE38Q	Init. Data Transfer In Transit Qty
SE39	Splitscreen Editor: (New)
SE39O	Splitscreen Editor: Program Compare
SE40	MP: Standards Maint. and Translation
SE61	R/3 Documentation
SE61D	Display of SAPScript Text
SE62	Industry Utilities
SE63	Translation: Initial Screen
SE63_OTR	Translation - OTR
SE64	Terminology
SE71	SAPscript form
SE72	SAPscript Styles
SE73	SAPscript Font Maintenance
SE74	SAPscript format conversion
SE75	SAPscript Settings
SE75TTDTGC	SAPscript: Change standard

	symbols
SE75TTDTGD	SAPscript: Display standard symbols
SE76	SAPscript: Form Translation
SE77	SAPscript Styles Translation
SE78	Administration of Form Graphics
SE80	Object Navigator
SE81	Application Hierarchy
SE82	Application Hierarchy
SE83	Reuse Library
SE83_START	Start Reuse Library
SE84	R/3 Repository Information System
SE85	ABAP/4 Repository Information System
SE89	Maintain Trees in Information System
SE8I	Lists in Repository Infosystem
SE90	Process Model Information System
SE91	Message Maintenance
SE92	New SysLog? Msg Maintenance as of 46A
SE92N	Maintain System Log Messages
SE93	Maintain Transaction Codes
SE94	Customer enhancement simulation
SE95	Modification Browser
SE95_UTIL	Modification Browser Utilities

SE97	Maintain transaction call authorization
SEARCH_SAP_MENU	Find in SAP Menu
SEARCH_USER_MENU	Find in User Menu
SECATT	Extended Computer Aided Test Tool
SECOCO	Control Composer
SECR	Audit Information System
SECSTO	Administration of Secure Memory
SELVIEW	Selection view maintenance
SEM_BEX	Business Explorer Analyzer
SEM_NAV	Business Explorer Navigator
SENG	Administration of External Indexes
SENGEXPLORER	Explorer Index Administration
SEO_PATTERN_GENE RATE	Update Pattern
SERP	Reporting: Change Tree Structure
SESS	Session Manager Menu Tree Display
SESSION_MANAGER	Session Manager Menu Tree Display
SESS_START_OBJECT	Start an Object
SEU_DEPTYPE	Maintain dependency types
SEU_INT	Object Navigator

Please visit www.sapcookbook.com to read more about other books in our SAP Interview Questions, Answers, and Explanations series:

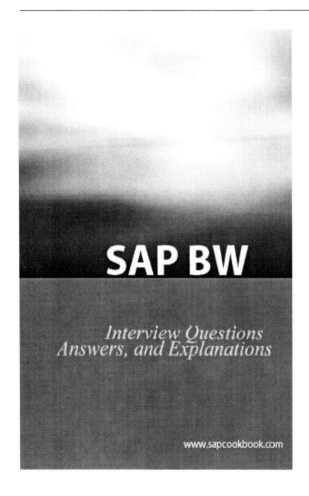

CPSIA information can be obtained at www.ICGtesting.com
Printed in the USA
BVOW021240130213

313128BV00002B/401/A